SPANISH MISSION HASTINGS
STYLES OF FIVE DECADES

By Peter Shaw
Photographs by Peter Hallett

ART DECO TRUST
Napier, New Zealand

ACKNOWLEDGEMENTS
The publisher thanks the Hastings District Council for its support.

PHOTO ACKNOWLEDGEMENTS
Unless otherwise acknowledged, all photographs are by Peter Hallett.
Historical photographs were sourced from the Hawke's Bay Museum, the Alexander Turnbull Library, the Havelock North Library, the Hastings Central Public Library, the Cliff Press, the Harvey family, Anna McKenzie, Mr & Mrs Charles Gordon, Gerry van Asch, Paul Waite, the Gummer Family, Home & Building magazine and the Architectural Archive, University of Auckland.

First Published by Cosmos Publications 1991

Second Edition published by the Art Deco Trust 2006

Spanish Mission Hastings is a companion volume to
ART DECO NAPIER – STYLES OF THE THIRTIES
Fifth Edition published by the Art Deco Trust 2002

Book Design by Denise Wilkinson & Warren Sang.
Production by Robert McGregor.
Printed by Brebner Print Ltd.

ISBN 978-0-9582697-0-4.

FOREWORD

The Art Deco Trust is delighted to become the publisher of *Spanish Mission Hastings*, coinciding its launch with Hastings' **Fifty Years a City** celebrations.

The first edition appeared in 1991. In the 15 years since then awareness and appreciation of Hastings' inner city buildings have increased markedly. Many of them had to be re-photographed because they have now been painted in carefully considered colour schemes which have enhanced and drawn attention to their character. Towns and small cities in new world countries are not known for their architecture, but Hastings, like Napier, is fortunate to have a townscape which relates to a particular era, with the cohesiveness and harmony that results. That these styles are seen in such concentration makes them even more remarkable and Hastings' CBD has a richness which has for too long been under-valued.

It is necessary to repeat here the acknowledgements of the first edition, for this book owes as much to the following people as its predecessor. James Morgan, then editor of the Hawke's Bay Herald Tribune (now Hawke's Bay Today), June Johnson of the Havelock North Library and Joan McCracken of the Alexander Turnbull Library all gave valuable assistance. Julia Grigg spent dusty hours among the old building permits held by the Hastings District Council, and Patrick Sherratt and Susan Hallett contributed vitally at all stages to the original photographing of the book. And the late Jeremy Dwyer, at the time mayor of the Hastings District Council, was supportive and encouraging of the publication. The present appreciation of these buildings is largely a result of his determination and vision.

This second edition has been made possible by the support of the present mayor, Lawrence Yule, and the Hastings District Council. Colin Hosford has assisted with research, and he, Cr Margaret Twigg and John Davidson have served on the Landmarks Liaison Committee. We have been grateful for the scholarly assistance of Paul Waite and to Judy Siers who cast an expert eye over the final proofs.

Lastly, of course, I must thank Peter Shaw for his revised text and his helpful comments, and Peter Hallett, who first suggested to me that we take over as publisher, and whose photographs so beautifully illustrate the book.

Robert McGregor
Executive Director
ART DECO TRUST

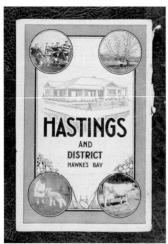

In 1929 Lovell and Painter, printers of Queen Street, Hastings were responsible for the production of a copiously illustrated Official Handbook of Hastings for Tourist, Sportsman and Settlers. Initiated by the then Hastings Borough Council, it was designed to draw visitors to a town which at this time was less well known than its nearby and older neighbour, Napier.

Taking a grandly omniscient view, the Handbook's opening pages emphasised the beauties of Hawke's Bay in a style which, although quaint by today's standards, nevertheless captured the essence of the place. It referred to the province's noble stretches of hills, to its blossoming orchard lands, to the vivid blueness of its river waters. Then, moving to Hastings' site in the Heretaunga Plains, it described the myriad streams which join the three rivers, Ngaruroro, Tukituki and Tutaekuri "... as they flow from the mountains to unite with a naturally fertile soil and a climate which the pagans would have thought was made according to the formula of their goddess of the harvest to make the district an ideal home for man and beast, and for everything that good land, water and sunshine can bestow."

The writer of this purple prose does not mention the fact that the former Maori owners, members of the Ngati Kahungunu tribe, had appreciated the qualities of the Heretaunga Plains long before the pakeha ever set foot on it. Although the swampy plains were not inhabited in pre-European times, they were a valuable source of food as well as flax and raupo, both useful for clothing and as building material.

It was these Maori inhabitants who, imagining a partnership of equal benefit to both races, initially encouraged pakeha to settle in central Hawke's Bay during the 1850s. They were adamant that the Heretaunga Plains remain in Maori ownership. As relations between the two races deteriorated following the outbreak of the Maori-Pakeha Land Wars in other parts of New Zealand, Maori gradually became less willing to sell their land to settlers whose motives they now began to suspect. Finally in 1870 under circumstances of dubious legality the Heretaunga Plains passed out of Maori ownership. They did so as the price paid for peace in Hawke's Bay.

In 1867 a group of settlers led by Thomas Tanner was able first to lease and then in 1870 to purchase a total of 19,385 acres. Historian Mary Boyd called the Heretaunga Purchase "the most notorious example of a new method of direct purchase by private individuals introduced by the Government in 1865 to overcome Maori resistance to land-selling." In the following years, despite fears of war and outright confiscation of Maori land, a Maori Repudiationist Movement fought to have the disputed purchase declared fraudulent and overturned. It was unsuccessful.

The town of Hastings had its origin on land known by Maori name of Karamu. It was here that a railway station was built in 1873 on the line from Napier to Pakipaki. The land was officially owned by one Francis Hicks, who had earlier purchased a 100-acre block from Thomas Tanner. Despite a persistent local legend, it is unlikely that it was ever named Hicksville; instead the town commemorates Warren Hastings, the first British Governor-General of India, and thus it continued the imperial colonial associations which had already led to the naming of Napier, Clive and Havelock.

In 1873 a town plan was produced for an auction of sections which began on July 8th. The first day of the sale concluded with a champagne evening put on by Francis Hicks. Settlers returned the following day to bid even more keenly for property. The swamps were drained, the flax, scrub and fern burned off to create pasture. Now a grid-like pattern was imposed on it and streets given names which recalled the English origins of the settlers. Sales continued through the following decade as the original landowners were forced to subdivide by an increasingly unfavourable economic climate.

Unlike Napier, which because of its location quickly took on the appearance of an English seaside resort, Hastings developed during the 1870s and 1880s

Stoneycroft, one of the earliest surviving two-storyed villas in the area, was built for W. Birch of Erewhon Station on the Napier Taihape Road as a convenient town house.

The wooden St Matthews Church (1877). Its façade was deliberately built to resemble the west front of Westminster Abbey.
Hastings Central Library, Old Hastings Collection.

The Albert Hotel as it is today.

as a service town for its extensive rural hinterland. By 1882 the population of Hastings numbered 617 and there were 131 freehold landowners living in the growing town. The greatest period of expansion took place after 1885 when Hastings rapidly developed a modest commercial area around its station.

Architecturally, it had the appearance of many similarly sized New Zealand settler towns. Houses in the cottage or villa styles were built in wood by the firm of Knight Brothers which had opened in 1876. By far the most substantial of these was the enormous two storyed veranda-ed villa built at Riverslea by Thomas Tanner. A Post Office, Fire Station, and the Hastings District School all followed as did an Anglican wooden church of St Matthew which welcomed its first congregation in 1877 to a Gothic styled building whose façade bore a distinct resemblance to the west front of Westminster Abbey.

During the following two decades many businesses were established. Hotels with promenading verandahs were built, the most commodious being the Hastings Hotel, designed by the Napier architect W. A. Dugleby, who duplicated dining and sitting rooms in the interests of class demarcation. The Albert Hotel which also dates from this period, is the only survivor. A Town Hall, more churches, and banks in the classical style favoured for such buildings at the time followed. They were mostly the work of builders who understood wood and whose designs reflected the fashionable styles of the day. Because most of early Hastings was built in wood it is not surprising that few original buildings survive today. In February 1893 a particularly serious fire destroyed much of the town's central business district.

It was not until the turn of the century that architects began to work in Hastings, by which time there were citizens wealthy enough to afford the services of such professionals. One of the first was George Sollitt (1834–1912) a Yorkshireman who set up practice in Hastings in 1890 from Christchurch where he had been a general contractor since his arrival at Lyttelton on board the Lady Jocelyn in 1879. He shrewdly perceived that the services of an architect would be required by wealthy landed Hawke's Bay settlers either anxious to upgrade their original dwellings or to build new homes on smaller land holdings in the wake of the Seddon government's imposition of a land tax which made larger holdings uneconomical. Sollitt soon established the flourishing architectural practice of Sollitt and Allan.

In 1895 a small church, designed by Dugleby, which now survives as a schoolroom, was replaced by Sollitt's 1895 Church of the Sacred Heart in Heretaunga Street. This beautiful church burned down in 1992. Its foundation stone had been laid by Archbishop Redwood on 7 October 1894. Compared with 'Westminster Abbey' built nearly twenty years earlier, Sacred Heart was even more soaringly Gothic. Its central spire was supported by pointed corner buttresses and provided with pinnacles; its interior detailing showed that Sollitt was an expert in designing in wood, a skill which was to prove useful in attracting clients wishing to use his services as a domestic architect.

Only one of his large houses survives today while another, Waiterenui, although altered in the 1920s, still bears signs of his expertise. In 1899 he had designed an enormously extended single-storyed wooden villa at Horonui for H. M. Campbell, a newly married, wealthy man in his early twenties whose sociable personality no doubt determined his decision to incorporate a magnificent rimu-panelled billiard room and servants' quarters to accommodate a permanent staff of six. Horonui too fell victim to fire in 1998. The house was built on land originally a part of the much larger Poukawa Station established by his father, and was distinguished by a verandah stretching along the length of the house, giving panoramic views down a long valley towards the distant Hastings.

The Church of the Sacred Heart (1895) by George Sollitt and Allan was destroyed by fire in 1992.

The following year Sollitt designed Greenhill, at Raukawa Road, for Archibald McLean. In 1888 McLean had purchased 3,300 acres of the huge Maraekakaho Station from his employer and fellow clansman Sir Donald McLean who, already expert in land purchase negotiations in Taranaki and Hawke's Bay, had been ideally placed to acquire this land from Ngati Kahungunu in 1850. The house was spectacularly sited on a hill overlooking the Ngatarawa Plains whose 19,000 acres had been purchased from Maori during the 1860s. The architect, no doubt inspired by the site and his client's aspiration to be lord of all he surveyed, designed a three-storyed central viewing turret which dominated the villa. On a long verandah frequently interrupted by porticos are elaborately turned paired posts; shingled gables adorn a roof structure of enormous complexity; eaves are supported by brackets of widely varying types. Fireplaces, mouldings, carved woodwork and stained glass are all extremely ornate. Work on building the house took two years to complete, a panelled billiard room being added in 1901.

Horonui (1899–1900) by George Sollitt was an extended single storyed villa with a veranda along its garden front. It was destroyed by fire in 1998.

Her Majesty Queen Elizabeth, the Queen Mother with her hosts Gladys & Richard Hudson on the front steps at Greenhill in 1958.
N Z Herald/Weekly News Photograph, courtesy Anna Mackenzie

St Andrews Presbyterian Church (1906) was designed by C. T. Natusch in his favourite half-timbered Elizabethan manner.
Alexander Turnbull Library

After Archibald McLean's death in 1929 Greenhill passed to his daughter-in-law's family. The house came to national prominence in the summer of 1958 when for some days it accommodated Queen Elizabeth, the Queen Mother, who was photographed under the central portico carrying the inevitable bouquet, flanked by her hosts Richard and Gladys Hudson. Since 2002 a carefully renovated Greenhill has operated under the same name as a luxury lodge, its Buxton designed garden with a wisteria walk having been considerably restored and its spectacular site once more able to be fully appreciated.

Also working in Hawke's Bay at this time was Charles Tilleard Natusch (1859–1952) who had established a practice in Wellington in 1886 following his emigration from England. Like Sollitt, Natusch was devoted to wood. He became well known for large houses built in what is usually referred to as an Elizabethan style because it owes much to the fashion for Tudor domestic revivalist building in England during the latter years of the nineteenth century. Natusch was quick to appreciate its applicability in New Zealand, where there were abundant supplies of hardwood suitable for building.

At Matapiro his client was Walter Shrimpton, another early landowner who in 1872 had arrived in Hawke's Bay as a land valuer. In 1875 he and a partner purchased 22,000 acres of land from its previous Pakeha owners, and built a single-storyed house on a terrace near an old Ngati Upokoiri whare whakairo (carved meeting house). In 1902 he decided to engage C. T. Natusch to transform this house into a homestead, a process which took eight years to complete.

The result was a large emphatically symmetrical two-storyed house with half-timbered gables on either side of deep verandahs which served both storeys. Like both Horonui and Greenhill, its timber frame is clad with rusticated weatherboards, its roof is of corrugated iron. Timber ornamentation is much more restrained than on Sollitt's houses, reflecting a more modern approach to decoration, as the Art Nouveau stained glass windows above the magnificent staircase and on fanlights in sitting and bedrooms indicate.

Sollitt adopted the more old-fashioned view that quantity of detail is paramount, while Natusch preferred to please the eye by carefully varying the spacing of his verandah balustrading and keeping ornament to a minimum. His layout of the interior, while providing many formal rooms of generous proportions, is notable for its profusion of corridors, those for service functions being narrow and dark, while others for family use are wider and less gloomy. Approached by a long drive Matapiro is still surrounded by the superb gardens for which it has long been famous in the area.

C. T. Natusch in partnership with F. H. Frankland was also responsible in 1912 for a huge house called Tuna Nui. This property of 30,000 acres had been taken up by Captain Andrew Russell, who with his brother William had first come to New Zealand in 1857 as a member of the 58th Regiment. The 1912 house was built for Sir Andrew Hamilton Russell, who, following service with the British Army in India, had come to farm in New Zealand in 1892.

Tuna Nui is a timber-framed house set on concrete foundations, clad not in weatherboards but in two-inch thick stucco, with a Marseilles tiled roof. For insulation its interior walls are lined with powdered pumice on cedar slats, a procedure unusual in New Zealand but relatively common in the United States.

The rather surprising use both of this technique and of stucco by an architect well known for his allegiance to wood owes much to the fact that F. H. Frankland had been an architectural engineer in the U.S. before coming to New Zealand. The hand of C. T. Natusch is more clearly evident in the hall of this massive two-storyed house; it is rimu-panelled and conceived on an even grander scale than that at Matapiro. Tuna Nui is one of the first buildings in the Hastings area to depart significantly from the standard wooden villa type of domestic architecture found in towns all over New Zealand.

In the centre of Hastings a number of large buildings were constructed in brick and plaster rather than wood. Of these one of the most notable was the Grand Hotel designed by another local architect, C. A. Vautier, in a highly eclectic Edwardian Baroque manner. Few of Hastings' timber hotels had managed to survive the fires with which the town was all too often plagued. In these years no one imagined that the Grand or the 1909 Post Office, one of the most imposing designed by the Government Architect, John Campbell, would have to contend with an earthquake as massive of the one which destroyed them both in 1931. It is even more ironic that the city's last surviving brick Edwardian Baroque building, Penty and Lawrence's 1914 Union Bank of Australia, having survived the earthquake, was demolished by its owners, the ANZ Bank, as late as 1984.

A new St Matthew's Anglican Church, built to designs by C. J. Mountfort of Christchurch on the site of the old 'Westminster Abbey' and consecrated in

The Grand Hotel, designed by C. A. Vautier, Hawke's Bay's highest building at that time, did not survive the earthquake.
Alexander Turnbull Library, Auckland Star Collection

The impressive Hastings Post Office (1909), designed by John Campbell, the Government Architect.
Alexander Turnbull Library, Lovell Smith Collection

Virginia creeper soon covered Frederick de Jersey Clere's 1914 concrete additions to the original St Matthew's Church, designed in 1886 by C. J. Mountfort.
Alexander Turnbull Library, Radcliffe Collection

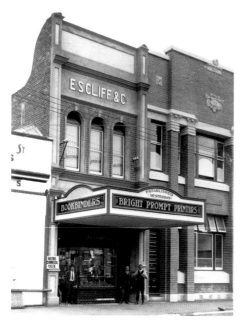

The Cliff Press Building and the Cotterill & Humphries Building designed by J. A. Louis Hay of Napier in 1915. Both are typical of the unstrengthened brick buildings which crumbled during the 1931 earthquake.
Alexander Turnbull Library

Queen Street in the mid 1920s.
John Murtagh Collection, Hastings

1886 had been considerably extended in 1914. The addition of a chancel, lady chapel, transept and tower built in an unusual variation of the original church's wooden Gothic was the work of Wellington architect Frederick de Jersey Clere. Its unpainted ferro-concrete construction supported by octagonal piers instead of buttresses may have given it a forbidding appearance but certainly ensured its survival in the earthquake. The church formerly possessed a higher tower which was lowered in 1931.

Noteworthy inside St Matthew's is the work of the eminent English stained glass artist Karl Parsons (1884–1934), whose 1914 five-light 'Adoration of the Blessed Virgin with Christ, Shepherds and the Magi' dominates the chancel. In 1926 Parsons made three additional windows for the Lady Chapel, each of them characterised by sumptuous colours, a highly worked surface and beauty of design. It is said that these owe their particular intensity of colour not only to his skill and reaction to seeing the medieval windows at Chartres Cathedral in 1924 but also to his understanding of the constant level of bright Hawke's Bay sunlight which would illuminate his glowing forms.

The Napier architect J. A. Louis Hay (1881–1948) also did some work in Hastings in this period and his brick office premises for Cotterill and Humphries in 1915, which did not survive in 1931, are an early example of the influence of the work of the great American architect Frank Lloyd Wright. Earlier, Hay, who had spent his apprenticeship years from 1896 serving articles in the Natusch office, designed wooden houses very much in the manner of his masters. Though not a thorough Domestic Revivalist he nevertheless seems to have favoured half-timbered gables on his otherwise conventional early villas. Like many architects familiar with ideas of domestic comfort illustrated in the English *Studio Magazine* in the first decade of the new century, he frequently specified the use of Art Nouveau stained glass windows and was fond of giving sitting rooms inglenook fireplaces.

In 1912 he designed a huge concrete house for Selwyn Chambers in the hills above Havelock North. Called Kopanga, it was built, unusually, in solid concrete and thus sustained only minor damage in the earthquake. Hay, struck by the panoramic views across the Heretaunga Plains, designed a north facing façade with deep verandahs and groups of large double-hung sash windows; the projecting verandah balustrades in concrete derive from C. T. Natusch's wooden ones but look clumsy by comparison. The upper storey's flattened central gable with its wide overhanging eaves already indicates Hay's familiarity with the Californian bungalow.

Plans and elevations of bungalows had been regularly appearing in *New Zealand Building Progress* magazine and were eagerly seized upon by architects looking for a way to escape the omnipresent villa. Kopanga shows that Hay, working on a large commission for a wealthy client, was prepared to try something new but was not yet able to dismiss his familiar way of working.

His even more massive Te Mahanga, designed for John Douglas at Poukawa in 1918, was constructed in brick and plaster and consequently collapsed entirely in 1931. Contemporary photographs reveal a house with a lower storey of plastered roughcast with a Natusch-like upper storey complete with half-timbered gables and long sleeping porches. These latter two features, in addition to the tiled roof and turret-room, were highly fashionable in the Hastings–Havelock North area at the time as the work of another architect clearly shows.

The prolific Hastings architect William Rush (1872–1965) was to use these features in creating a regional Hawke's Bay style. Born at Northhampton where he was articled to an architectural firm, he arrived in New Zealand in 1904 and in 1906 formed a partnership with E.T. James which lasted until 1914. This partnership, so the magazine *Progress* informed its readers in April 1911, "may be relied upon to give that artistic touch which makes a home of a house." Their most prominent building today is St. Luke's Church (1912), to which Warren and Mahoney in association with Paris Magdalinos added a steeple in 1998.

Attracted by the sunny climate, it was Rush who was the first of many Hawke's Bay architects to envisage the appropriateness of the Spanish Mission style to the region. He began tentatively, realising that it would be unwise for a new architect to contradict a prevailing fashion for Domestic Revivalism, but gradually he introduced elements of a Californian style which in time became acceptable to his clients.

The combination of features from both English Domestic Revival and Californian styles can best be seen on his own 1908 House at the top of Durham Drive, Havelock North. Called Ngawiwi, the Maori word used to translate his own surname, the house has villa-like squared bay windows with multi-paned fanlights above. The eaves of its main half-timbered gable project out in the fashionable Californian Bungalow manner; the rows of pointed exposed rafter ends underneath were also fashionable at the time and much used by

Front and rear views of the house, Te Mahanga which Louis Hay designed in 1918.
Louis Hay Album

W. J. Rush's HAWKE'S BAY COUNTRY HOUSE. The plans were published in *The Forerunner* in 1913, but it was never built.

McHardy House, Havelock North (1916), also by Rush. Sleeping porches were an essential feature of the architect's Havelock North houses.

Louis Hay. The house has a number of sleeping porches either of the more modern Californian Spanish arcaded variety, made in stucco, or balustraded with elaborately cut posts. During the two years that Rush and his family lived in this house the architect was suffering from tuberculosis. One of the main reasons for his advocacy of the sleeping porch from that time on was his adherence to the fashionable medical opinion that the condition of those with weak lungs would be helped by sleeping out of doors.

A competent watercolour painter and illustrator, he submitted plans and elevations to *The Forerunner*, the magazine published by Havelock residents interested in fostering discussion of religious, scientific and educational questions. In the edition for January 1911 he illustrated and wrote *A Home for the Simple Life*, advocating deep porches for sleeping and dressing as well as al fresco dining beneath wisteria-draped pergolas. Because his aim was to promote an outdoor lifestyle it is not surprising that the Californian style with arcaded verandahs and wide overhanging eaves should be deemed appropriate.

His Hawke's Bay Country House in *The Forerunner* of December 1913, planned around a courtyard, also has these features. Neither of these bungalows was ever built, clients tending to favour something more conventional such as the two-storyed McHardy House (1916), though it too was provided with a Californian verandah gable above its upper storey sleeping porch. A circular turreted open garden room forms an unexpected conclusion to the ground floor's verandah which stretches along the front of the house. Rush liked the effect of cream painted stucco walls, orange Marseilles tiled roofs and green painted window trim.

His work was not limited to domestic building. In 1911 for Woodford House at Havelock North he decided on an appropriately English model. Instead of the traditional Gothic school, he designed a building characterised by wide-angled, downward sweeping rooflines broken with dormer windows much in the manner of C. F. A. Voysey. Sloping chimney forms accentuated the resemblance while half-timbered gables acknowledged the fashionable English Domestic Revival. Again the walls were stuccoed and the rooflines tiled. The timbered hall with its scissor-trussed rafters is manorial; classrooms and the dining room were timber panelled to head height, their ceilings supported by heavy beams. Rush's school building at Woodford House succeeded in emphasising a domestic rather than an institutional character.

An early photograph of Woodford House as it looked soon after completion of the buildings designed by Rush in 1911.
Alexander Turnbull Library

In 1913 he also designed Heretaunga School, now called Hereworth, and the more innovative Iona College. Iona still exhibits the Spanish Mission character which Rush gave it in 1913 and which the architect Edmund Anscombe fully respected in his restoration of the school's buildings after they were seriously weakened following the earthquake. It is interesting that Rush was working on Iona in the same period as Atkinson and Abbott designed what remains New Zealand's largest and most impressive building in the Spanish Mission style, Auckland Grammar School.

Iona's arcaded cloisters recall those of the Spanish Missions of California; the main building's central tower has round-headed windows reminiscent of Mission bell towers; overhanging eaves are supported on ornamental brackets which, like Auckland Grammar's, owe something to the Californian Craftsman bungalow also popular at this time. Typically Spanish Mission too is a balcony with a set of three windows above the library's sun-trap bow window. The three windows have rounded fanlights and are separated by the characteristic barley twist columns which were later to become such a common feature on Hastings' post earthquake buildings. A comparison of photographs of the original buildings with those taken after the 1931 restoration reveals that these windows and columns are not the work of Rush and James but of Edmund Anscombe who, in adding a storey above the original bow windowed library in 1931, added to Iona's Spanish Mission character details which were to re-appear on his 1932 department store for Westerman Brothers in Heretaunga Street.

No survey of the architecture of this area would be complete without mention of the Havelock North houses of J. W. Chapman-Taylor (1878–1958.) This architect came to Havelock North in 1913 three years after having returned from England where he had visited some of the main protagonists of the Arts and Crafts movement. Like Rush, Chapman-Taylor saw the possibility of adapting English architectural ideas to the New Zealand climate.

The circumstances which led him to move from Wellington to Havelock and to build a number of houses there are unusual. In 1908 a Hastings businessman, Reginald Gardiner, gathered a group of prominent local citizens to read and discuss literary matters. Gradually they developed this into a highly active cultural society called The Havelock Work specifically to encourage performances of music and drama. It was these people who produced *The Forerunner*, the magazine to which both Rush and Chapman-Taylor were

The Spanish influenced buildings at Iona College by Rush in their original form, dating from 1913.
Radcliffe Collection, Alexander Turnbull Library

Iona photographed in 1931 during the course of the restoration work undertaken by Edmund Anscombe.
Alexander Turnbull Library

Designed by J. W. Chapman-Taylor in 1915, the Transformer House, Havelock North, was originally commissioned by the Town Board for the village's first electricity supply. It subsequently became a public convenience and in 1994 was remodelled to incorporate the Havelock North Visitor Information Centre.
Havelock North Library

Havelock North's Village Hall (1912), by W. J. Rush, was unfortunately demolished in 1997.

occasional contributors. The same people were responsible for raising money by organising an Old English Village Fete in 1911 and a Shakespearian Pageant in 1912 to finance the building of Havelock's Village Hall.

Both Reginald Gardiner and his wife Ruth were interested in meditation as a means of gathering wisdom about the spiritual and philosophical truths which lay behind the more formalised religion of the various Christian churches. In 1910 a visiting priest from the Anglican monastic order, The Community of the Resurrection, became acquainted with The Havelock Work's interests and it was through him in 1912 that Dr Robert William Felkin arrived in Havelock North.

This remarkable man was a graduate of both Edinburgh and Heidelburg universities. Inspired by a childhood meeting with Dr David Livingstone he became an explorer who travelled widely in Africa and was reputed to be the first man accurately to measure the Pigmy people of the Congo. He was also a pioneer student of tropical diseases, a staunch Anglican and a tireless student of esoteric spiritual knowledge. For the small Havelock North community which Reginald Gardiner had gathered around him, Dr Felkin's presence was inspirational. During the three months which he spent in the town of less than five hundred inhabitants he established a branch of the London-based hermetic Order of the Golden Dawn, called Stella Matutina (Morning Star). He gave the Havelock chapter the name of Smaragdum Thalasses (Emerald Seas) and initiated its first adherents to the order's secret rituals before returning to England. By 1916, encouraged in the belief that the climate in Hawke's Bay would be good for his now failing health, Dr Felkin returned to Havelock North with his second wife Harriot and Ethelwyn, his daughter by a previous marriage. He set up practice as a general practitioner and, until his death in 1926, supervised the order he had founded.

Before they left New Zealand, Dr Felkin and his wife had been generously provided with a piece of land below his own property at Tauroa by Mason Chambers. The architect appointed was Chapman-Taylor who then came from Wellington with his own family to work in Havelock North. The house, called Whare Ra, is unusual because here the architect was to some extent obliged to depart from his Arts and Crafts principles in order to accommodate his client's specifically religio-philosophical as well as architectural requirements.

It is oriented along an east-west axis because this is the same direction as Moses had cast his tent. Beneath the house is a large rectangular concrete basement which houses the Temple, the eastern end of which culminates in a seven-sided vault whose walls, doors and ceiling are to this day still covered with brightly coloured astrological, kabbalistic and other symbols.

On its upper level the plastered brick, roughcast-finished house looks more conventional. Much less obviously English than Chapman-Taylor's other houses of this period, it has the deep verandahs so common in Hastings and Havelock houses. Its flattened gables give the exterior of the house a Californian appearance but inside Arts and Crafts hand-adzed woodwork door fittings, exposed jarrah beams and a baronial fireplace all indicate that Chapman-Taylor was given the opportunity to demonstrate his affection for the hand-crafted medievalising features to which he was always devoted. The house was divided into a family living area, at the southern end, which had its own entrance and was joined by a corridor leading to bedrooms and eventually to the more formal drawing room from which the order's robed adherents were led blindfolded down a circuitous staircase to an antechamber connected to the Temple.

One particularly innovative aspect of the design was the architect's ingenious solution to the problem of darkness in rooms behind a deep verandah. By operating sliding panels, light entered the rooms through glass tiles which were placed in the roof. So that Dr Felkin's consulting rooms could be situated close by, William Rush designed an annexe to Whare Ra, which was later removed and now sits at the bottom of the drive which leads up to the house.

In 1917 the house called Turama (Lantern) which Chapman-Taylor had designed in 1916 for Reginald Gardiner was built in Duart Road, just below Whare Ra. Turama is perhaps less unusual as an example of Chapman-Taylor's work though it is more extensively decorated in carved Christian and Rosicrucian symbols than Whare Ra. From the evidence of an article extolling the importance of ritual in revealing inner truth which Chapman-Taylor contributed to *The Forerunner* in 1912, he too was a member of the inner circle which gathered around Dr Felkin and Reginald Gardiner.

In 1919 Chapman-Taylor built Oak Trees, which he described as "a workshop fitted as a temporary dwelling" in Campbell Street as a home for his family while he built Sunborne on a section just above it in Duart Road, Havelock North. The larger house is distinguished by an open garden room which the architect had not originally designed but added during the

Sunborne, Chapman-Taylor's own house in Havelock North was completed in 1920. The kitchen sink-bench and the bath were of concrete, finished with bottle green brick-shaped tiles.

course of construction. Its floor is a reinforced concrete slab and the walls an extraordinary honeycomb construction of empty petrol cans set between layers of reinforced concrete.

Like Rush and others concerned with The Havelock Work and its associated spiritual quests, Chapman-Taylor believed that people should live in close association with the outdoors. He planned his own house so that sun and fresh air could enter all its interior spaces. The plan also emphasised the importance of close-knit family social functions; dining, sitting by the fire or, in summer, in the garden room. The inglenook around the fireplace bore a motto "O ye fire and heat, bless ye the Lord, praise him and magnify Him forever."

The other eminent New Zealand architect to work in the Havelock area was W. H. Gummer (1884–1966). His association with the wealthy landowning Chambers family came about as the result of his friendship with Maurice Chambers who from 1919 to 1926 lived at Louis Hay's Kopanga. Maurice's wife was Miriama Chambers (nee Batley) the sister of Te Oira Arani Batley, who married W. H. Gummer whom she had first met at Tauroa while still a pupil at Woodford House. The close association between Gummer and members of the Chambers family was to result in his building four magnificent houses between 1916 and 1935.

The first, Tauroa, dates from 1916 and was built for Mason and Madge Chambers as a replacement for their wooden house which had burned to the ground in 1914. From the first, Mason Chambers determined on an earthquake and fireproof home and immediately engaged Gummer, already a highly rated young architect with experience in the London office of Sir Edwin Lutyens and that of Daniel Burnham in Chicago. On returning to New Zealand in 1913 Gummer had become the Auckland partner in the Wellington-based firm of Hoggard and Prouse. The correspondence between the architect and his client reveals that in 1914 Gummer produced at least three different plans for the new Tauroa which, in 1916, was eventually built with double brick walls with a cavity between. Ferro-concrete pillars and beams added to the strength of the house which was finished in white stucco. Timber is either jarrah, because of its slow burning properties, or kauri.

Tauroa is one of New Zealand's most distinguished houses. In plan it is adventurous; all of its rooms radiate along two axes from a point at the base of a staircase which sweeps up on both sides of a circular hall. This plan also

Guests at Tauroa for the wedding of Maurice Chambers and Miriama Batley in 1923.
Hawke's Bay Museum

determines the unusual proportions of some of the rooms which back on to the hall. The dining room, for instance, has a curved wall which necessitated the designing of special furniture. Again the relationship between inside and outside was exploited, many of Tauroa's rooms opening either on to pergolas or porches. The local fetish for sleeping outside seems not to have been confined to clients of Louis Hay and William Rush.

Individual touches of craftsmanship are everywhere. The owner's initials are emblazoned on the finger plates of door furniture; in the dining room a beaten copper hood above the fireplace carries a Latin inscription: "Benedicite ignis et aestus domino, laudate et super exaltate cum in secula" which translates as "Bless fire and warmth in the name of the Lord. Praise and exalt Him on high for ever." This inscription is remarkably similar to the motto which adorned Chapman-Taylor's fireplace, a coincidence no doubt explainable by the fact that both men were closely associated with Dr Robert Felkin and his Order.

It is significant that the houses designed by Rush, Gummer, and Chapman-Taylor for members of the Order of the Golden Dawn closely reflected the spiritual concerns of their clients. For both, an interest in the relationship between the physical and the metaphysical went hand in hand with a respect for truth to materials and the values of honest craftsmanship. The philosophical concerns of Mason Chambers, Reginald Gardiner and other followers of Dr Felkin had precise architectural counterparts in these doctrines of the Arts and Crafts movement. Tauroa owes much to an English Arts and Crafts-derived devotion to fine workmanship. Local craftsmen hand-wrought the jarrah bannister as well as its ornate iron supports. In the dining room tiny bronze figurines appear to slide down the light cords; the library's floor-to-ceiling bookcases have specially designed shelves which slope outward to form convenient reading surfaces.

Tauroa also demonstrates the transition between its architect's allegiance to English Arts and Crafts models and the Beaux Arts classicism which was to become so evident in his commercial buildings of the 1920s. His favourite fasces motif decorates the ceiling in the library; a Doric frieze defines the dado in the music room; the motif of a circle within a square is found at the tops of doors; the cornice of the dining room ceiling consists of bands of dentils.

Gummer's growing preference for restrained classically-derived detailing is everywhere apparent. The extensive glazed area of the hall contains clear leaded

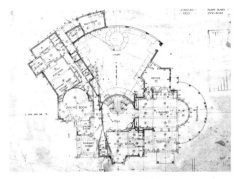

Tauroa's ground floor plan radiates from the base of the stair, a solution entirely novel for New Zealand at the time though one familiar to Gummer from Lutyens' planning experiments.
The Architecture Archive, University of Auckland and the Gummer Family

glass panels rather than the colourful floral Art Nouveau arabesques to which Louis Hay, for instance, remained devoted until the geometries of Frank Lloyd Wright's stained glass work made their inevitable impact on his decorative work.

Efficiency rather than craftsmanship led to the provision of a centralised vacuum cleaning system at Tauroa but this piece of domestic sophistication never operated because the ship transporting its electric motor was sunk during its wartime voyage to New Zealand.

The exterior of Tauroa is equally extraordinary. Its many shuttered windows give it a Georgian appearance while the upper storey balconies refer to the persistent Californian Spanish influence which was already becoming such a pronounced feature of the regional architecture of Hastings and Havelock. In a touch that is pure Spanish Mission, there is even an aperture designed to house a small bell in the wall of one of the wings. Distinctly modern for the time is the house's flat roof, obscured behind outlined parapets of varying heights.

Gummer's next Hawke's Bay house, originally called Craggy Range but now known as Belmount, was built between 1918 and 1919 for William Van Asch who had purchased a part of the Tukituki Station in 1913. Although certain aspects of the house's design remained unresolved upon its completion, Craggy Range represents its architect's earliest attempt to produce something which owed less to specific historical styles than to the modern English architecture with which he became familiar during his years of travel between 1908–1913.

Craggy Range's geometric rigour shows that Gummer must have been familiar with the 1908 house called Upmeads designed by Edgar Wood, an English architect who was initially the leading Arts and Crafts architect in the north of England but who by 1908 was one of the so-called English Free School. He had experimented with "uncraftsman-like" concrete, as did Chapman-Taylor and Gummer in New Zealand.

Both Upmeads and Craggy Range are exposed brick houses but Gummer chose to reveal his use of concrete by means of a string course to mark the distinction between the two storeys and in the heavy garden frontage with arcaded concrete balcony above. This overbearing feature upsets the proportions of the cubic forms which are otherwise such a distinctive feature of all elevations. Like both Wood and Lutyens, Gummer used a great variety of sizes of metal-framed windows, irregularly disposed over the façades. Again, as at Tauroa, the flat roof is hidden by a shallow parapet which steps up and down as the roof line varies. Like Tauroa the service area at the rear of the house is angled out and away from its main elevation and there is the same profusion of balconies and oddly shaped chimneys.

Inside Craggy Range the modernistic austerity of design persists. The dining room's brick fireplace is severely geometric; the billiard room is lined with exposed brick, the hall and library with Queensland maple; the staircase which ascends in the centre of the house has an unusually large number of turns and the first landing has a seat set into the wall to permit a moment of rest during the ascent.

Craggy Range was exceptional for its time, there being no New Zealand precedent for its unashamedly modern appearance. Gummer's English sources are clear; it is likely that, having travelled in the USA in 1913, he was familiar with contemporary Californian domestic architecture which was moving away from the excesses of Spanish Mission to something more restrainedly geometric. It has been only recently that Craggy Range received the attention it deserves, probably because of its remote though magnificent location looking straight at Te Mata Peak across the Tukituki Valley.

Gummer's two later Hawke's Bay houses, Arden (1926) and Te Mata (1935) were again built for members of the Chambers family. Arden, originally the home of Maurice and Miriama Chambers, is an elegant composition built of reinforced concrete and brickwork with a plaster finish. Interior joinery is totara. In conception the house exhibits many similarities with Spanish Modern houses in California, which combined a restrained use of Spanish features with a more pared back approach to detailing. Both Gummer and C. R. Ford, his partner since 1923 in what was already by 1926 New Zealand's premier architectural practice, had travelled in California. Ford spent the first six months of 1923 there on what his passport described as a "study and observation" tour. The photograph album he assembled on his return indicates an intense enthusiasm for a more modern Spanish Mission-influenced domestic architecture rather than for the over-decorated buildings of the first decade of the century. His interest lay in the work of contemporary architects who pursued more subtle allusions to California's Mission background.

The drawings for Arden indicate that the design concept was Gummer's and that the structural solutions involved were in the capable hands of C. R. Ford. Also involved was the practice's senior draughtsman, Gordon Wilson. He had been employed by Hoggard, Prouse and Gummer since 1918, was to become

The front of Craggy Range, probably in the 1920s.
Gerry van Asch Collection

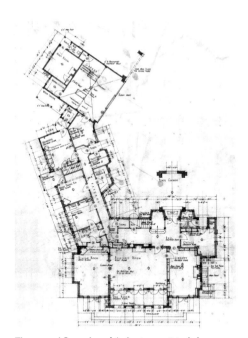

The ground floor plan of Arden is surprisingly large and irregular given the modest symmetry of its front elevation.
The Architecture Archive, University of Auckland and the Gummer Family

The original elevation of Arden, showing a pitched roof which was subsequently replaced by a flat one.
The Architecture Archive, University of Auckland and the Gummer Family

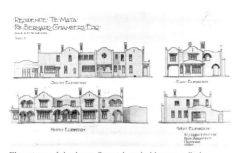

Elevations of the large Spanish-styled house called Te Mata, designed by W. J. Rush in 1920 and which collapsed in the 1931 earthquake. All that survives today are the water-colour drawings and the brick garden walls.

a partner at Gummer and Ford in 1928 and, later still, the New Zealand Government Architect.

Arden's symmetrical façade is characterised by a group of round-headed, fan-lit French doors; above, an open balcony leads back to covered porches off bedrooms. The house's west facing elevation incorporates an exterior staircase leading up to the flat roof upon which it was once intended to build a swimming pool. There is also an elegant little Juliet balcony. Like its predecessors, the detailing of Arden was given a distinctive unifying geometric motif which is best seen on the upper portion of the garden façade but is also used extensively inside, notably on the balusters of the main staircase. The porte cochère designed by Gummer in 1926 was not built until 1985 when the house's owners used the architect's plans to complete this important feature of his original conception.

The restraint with which Gummer and Ford incorporated a number of Spanish Mission features is characteristic of their work. By contrast William Rush's 1920 design for Te Mata, Bernard Chambers' house which crumbled to the ground in the 1931 earthquake, was fussily insistent in its heavy handed reference to a Spanish Mission style which had long since been superseded in both California and New Zealand.

From the architect's surviving watercolour elevations it is clear that Rush's huge stuccoed brick house sported the whole range of arcaded balconies, porches and doorways, groups of windows with bracketed hoods, parapeted gables as well as a brick-outlined bull's-eye window and an oriel window. Early photographs show that some of the arcaded verandah openings were able to be shaded with canvas blinds designed to protect sleepers from being awoken by early morning sun. Rush seems to have adopted a policy of including as many features as possible on his façades. The result of such an assemblage of references to Spanish Mission style was a house lacking any sense of unity.

However, this was something with which Gummer and Ford emphatically provided their client in 1935 when a new Te Mata was built. While the exterior's shuttered windows and tiled roof continued the Californian Spanish theme, interior planning and detailing are more conventionally neo-Georgian in approach. There are considerable asymmetries in its irregular arrangement of windows, porches and balconies; porches are now supported on slim wooden square columns and a balcony decorated with a wooden lattice balustrade.

Generally, restraint is the hallmark of Gummer and Ford's Te Mata. There is an impressive entrance hall at the centre of the house containing a staircase and large patterned clear glass windows. Rooms are disposed in the formal Georgian manner on either side of the central hall; downstairs rooms lead directly from one to the next while upstairs they are entered along corridors on either side of a landing at the top of the stairs. The Queensland maple panelling in the dining room, door surrounds in maple or walnut and an arched set of double doors, formerly the entry to Rush's Te Mata, were re-used from the earlier house. As usual, the highest standards of craftsmanship characterise every aspect of the new Te Mata's construction.

Gummer's private houses for a landed elite were relatively inaccessible to the public and remain so today. In Hastings itself it was rare to find buildings of such extravagance, though after 1907, when the break-up of the Pepper Estate occurred, some fine houses were built in the vicinity of Duke, York and Fitzroy Streets. In York Street Rush designed a large two-storeyed house for the Newbigen family in 1912. In 1914 an unknown architect was employed to design the Cato House for a client who had seen a picture of an English house in a book and wanted to have something similar built in Hastings. Called St Brigid's, the house is unusual in having a sun-trap plan, something which Chapman-Taylor had already used a number of times.

In the same year the young Hastings architect Albert Garnett (1878–1956) designed the Beatson House in York Street using the now familiar English model Rush had popularised. In 1911 and 1914 respectively he proved that he was prepared to desert this model in favour of the single-storeyed Californian bungalow when he produced the large homesteads Torran and Glen Aros in Raukawa Road for landowners occupying sections of what was formerly McLean's Maraekakaho Estate. Glen Aros has recently been refurbished and further enlarged with the addition of a separate wing; the garden too has been extended.

Typically for the time, Garnett's stylistic repertoire also encompassed Art Deco, as the extraordinary 1936 Atkins House in Pepper Street unmistakeably demonstrates. It was built for Percy Atkins, a well known Hawke's Bay jockey, who rode for businessman and racehorse owner Sir Robert Kerridge, whose Art Deco holiday home at Gisborne had been designed the previous year by local architects Burr and Mirfield. Such was the international appeal of the style

The pre-earthquake Te Mata, designed by Rush.
Collection Mr & Mrs Charles Gordon.

Two of the fine two-storeyed homes in the vicinity of Cornwall Park.
Above: the Cato house (1914–15) called St Brigid's is the work of an unknown English architect whose design the owner had seen in a magazine and had replicated in Hastings.
Below: The Beatson house (1914) by Albert Garnett shows how carefully the architect had absorbed the work of English domestic architects, despite his provision of distinctly antipodean sleeping porches.

The Hastings Methodist Church, designed in what was described as "an indifferent style of Gothic" by Albert Garnett in 1912.
Alexander Turnbull Library

Albert Garnett's Glenalvon (1927).

The date of construction and name of the architect for The Tourist Motors and Farming Company's petrol station on the corner of Queen and Market Streets is unknown. The building was demolished c.1970.
The Hawke's Bay Branch of the Vintage Car Club of New Zealand

that it was easily possible for architects to obtain material illustrating houses that shared the proliferation of rounded corners on cantilevered overhanging verandas, walls, steps, windows and parapets. The uniformity of the house's streamlined horizontality, its chrome balustrading and chamfered and stepped low wall make it a classic of the region. Inside woodwork has been restored and rooms furnished with appropriate items of period furniture collected by the current owners.

Albert Garnett's career lasted well into the mid 1950s. Although details of his training are unknown, he was assisted in his rise to early prominence by being the eldest son of James Garnett, a well known builder in the area who had been elected Mayor of Hastings in 1911. Between 1921 and 1924 Albert Garnett himself was a member of the Hastings Borough Council. Later, in partnership with Harold Davies and Eric Phillips, Garnett was a member of the town's most reputable and prolific architectural practice.

In 1912 he designed a new Methodist church in what the *Hastings Standard* described as "an indifferent style of Gothic," but there were greater things in store for him. In 1911 his father, during his term as mayor, negotiated the purchase of land on the corners of Heretaunga and Eastbourne Streets on which the council proposed to build a municipal building, shops, offices and a theatre.

By 1914 the town was ready to proceed and the architect Henry Eli White (1877–1952), already eminent in Wellington for his 1912 St James Theatre and soon to become known throughout Australasia as an innovative theatre designer, was appointed to carry out the design. White was ultimately to design only the Municipal Theatre in Hastings. A competition was held for the design of the Municipal Buildings but only architects practising within three miles of the Hastings Post Office were invited to submit proposals. This effectively excluded any Napier architects from entering the competition. From the eight submissions Albert Garnett was chosen as winner by the judge, Wellington architect Joshua Charlesworth.

White's Municipal Theatre was built first. To this day it remains Hastings' largest and most significant Spanish Mission building and one of New Zealand's finest theatres. The St James in Wellington is an opulent Edwardian Baroque structure; his masterpiece, Sydney's State Theatre was to be Gothic in inspiration. The Hastings Municipal Theatre has a Spanish Mission exterior but is lavishly decorated inside with motifs which indicate White's familiarity with the work of continental Art Nouveau architects and designers, particularly the Austrian Secessionist Josef Maria Olbrich who designed the highly influential 1897–88 Secession Building in Vienna.

For Henry Eli White consistency of exterior and interior style was not an issue. His theatres were to be lavishly decorated palaces of entertainment rather than architecturally correct monuments. Designed to seat 1400, the auditorium of the Municipal, as with all White's theatres, was notable for its uninterrupted sight lines, fine acoustics and excellent ventilation. For him the absence of "wretched pillars" was essential so he utilised his considerable engineering skills to design a steel framed cantilever system which ensured that both circle and balcony were visibly supported by just one slender steel column. In a characteristically forthright interview published in *The Theatre Magazine* of August 1914 White spoke of his objection to the way in which in the past theatres had been designed as if the stage was all-important but accommodation for actors too often neglected. This too he remedied in the Municipal Theatre. Despite the extravagance of decoration in all his theatres, White was emphatic that the "three great essentials … clear vision … a perfect acoustic … a scheme of ventilation…" came first. In fact it is likely that having solved these technical problems to his own satisfaction he used pattern books as the source for his decorative embellishments. The catalogue of the first great Exhibition of Modern Decorative Arts held at Turin, Italy in 1902 was a mine of information about Art Nouveau and Jugendstil art and provided architects all over the world with details of up-to-date styles. On the exteriors of his two Brisbane theatres White had already used the swirling tendrils and sinuous stem-like forms seen first on Olbrich's Secession House, later developed and popularised at Turin by such Italian designers as Raimondo D'Aronco and Giuseppe Velati-Bellini. More restrained in Hastings, New Zealand, White nevertheless swathed the boxes on either side of the stage of the Municipal Theatre with similar motifs.

The full repertoire of Spanish Mission decoration enlivened the plastered exterior façade of the Municipal Theatre. There are arched doors and windows, a balcony, broken columns, an ornamental balustrade, symmetrically placed long windows topped by bracketed window hoods and tiled roofed towers at each end. The Municipal Theatre is now a building of international significance not only because of the sophistication of its construction but also because of a decorative scheme which places it in a specific period of time in the history of design.

The Municipal Theatre also functioned for many years as a cinema. This photograph was taken when Rudolf Valentino's movie 'The Sheik' was screened in the early 1920s.
Hawke's Bay Museum

Renamed the Hawke's Bay Opera House, it was reopened in 2006 after an extensive refurbishment that deliberately drew on White's own eclectic mix of Secession and Spanish Mission elements. This included a magnificent painted ceiling in the main auditorium by artists Roz Paterson and Tina Carter, appropriately alluding to the work of Gustav Klimt who in 1902 had painted the *in situ* Beethoven frieze in Olbrich's Secession building in Vienna.

Next door, Garnett's Municipal Building displays the same eclectic qualities which marked his 1915 designs for shops in Heretaunga Street for Kilford and Ebbett, J. Hannah and for R. Warren. None of these remains today but the surviving drawings show that the architect was devoted to the kinds of heavy projecting decorative features which were to prove so dangerous in the 1931 earthquake. These simple structures were decorated with a profusion of cornices, curved window hoods, steeped parapets and open balustrades, some classical in inspiration, others showing evidence of acquaintance with the Turin exhibition catalogue. The 1914 building known today as Credit House in Queen Street is almost certainly his work, although no plans survive to prove the matter beyond doubt.

The Municipal Building, vacated by the Council in 1977, comprised ground floor shops and a main entrance on Heretaunga Street which led to a spacious vestibule and upstairs to the Assembly Hall; the Council Chamber had a separate entrance on Eastbourne Street. In the centre of the building is a tower with a tiled roof which forms a strong visual relation to the towers of the Municipal Theatre; this was used as a card room when dances were held in the Assembly Hall. At first floor level a balcony surrounds the whole structure; it projects out over the main entrance to form a space able to be used on civic ceremonial occasions.

To the architectural purist the exterior of the Municipal Building is perhaps confused, but such an eclectic approach was highly fashionable at the time it was built. In 1917 when it opened it would have appeared the height of fashion and a worthy demonstration of the town's growing commercial importance. It is thus a noteworthy survivor of a period of Hastings architecture which the earthquake all but wiped out. With the Municipal Theatre it forms a unique architectural heritage precinct which is now guaranteed permanent preservation as the result of work that commenced in 2006 to restore the former Council Chamber, now the Shakespeare Room, and the Assembly Hall.

Henry Eli White's Municipal Theatre, damaged but able to be restored, stands tall above the ruins of Garnett's Methodist Church opposite. Although the over hanging eaves on the two towers appear undamaged they were perceived as a potential hazard and reduced in width during restoration after the earthquake.
Alexander Turnbull Library, S. C. Smith Collection

Garnett was responsible in 1924 for the premises known today as Poppelwell's, originally built for Fitzpatrick & Co. Its Spanish flavour derives from the overhanging cordova-tiled eaves which, like the similar one on the Municipal Theatre, dominate the upper section of the building. Here the architect used patterns in relief brickwork to contrast with the white plastered façade. His elegant Villa d'Este shops and apartments, designed in 1929, were demolished following the earthquake in 1931, but later rebuilt in strengthened form to the original design.

Hastings' Spanish Mission character was firmly established before the earthquake. Even architects from outside Hastings respected the town's growing enthusiasm for the style. Wellington architects Clere and Williams were in 1920 to employ some restrained use of Spanish Mission features for their picture theatre named The Cosy, which did not survive the earthquake. So too did George Penlington, when he designed the administration block for Hastings Boys' High School in 1926. The Public Works Department in Wellington even authorised the importation of its roof tiles from Spain. Strengthening and renovation in 1979 has ensured the preservation of this notable building.

The 3rd of February 1931 was a fateful day for the whole of Hawke's Bay. Hastings, with a population of 11,000, suffered serious damage and loss of life. The swaying motion of the forces which rocked the ground in both towns had immediate effect on masonry buildings which simply crumbled. The steel reinforcing beams used in many buildings were inadequately attached to the brick walls they supported so they too collapsed. Only reinforced concrete buildings survived, most of them requiring attention as the result of cracking. Overhanging pediments, parapets and verandahs plummeted to the ground killing or seriously injuring people who rushed outside when they realised the magnitude of what was happening around them. After-shocks which went on for some days after the main earthquake continued to weaken those buildings which had not completely collapsed already. Hastings, earlier in its history known as the Town of Blazes, was fortunate in that the fires which followed the earthquake were quickly extinguished, unlike those in Napier.

The most imposing and prominent survivor was the Hawke's Bay Farmers' Building, designed by Edmund Anscombe (1873–1948) in 1928. With W. H. Gummer and J. W. Chapman-Taylor, Anscombe is, in national terms, the most eminent architect to have worked in Hastings. Born in England he arrived

Garnett's Villa d'Este apartments in Heretaunga Street had to be dismantled and rebuilt after the earthquake.
Hawke's Bay Museum

The interior of the Tea Rooms in the Hawke's Bay Farmers' Building, Hastings, reproduced from 'MODERN ARCHITECTURAL SERVICE as Practised by Edmund Anscombe and Associates.'
The Cliff Press, Hastings 1934

The bells of the Post Office tower were deposited
unceremoniously on to Queen Street during the
earthquake.
Alexander Turnbull Library

The single-storyed Westerman & Co building of 1921
had to be completely demolished after the earthquake.
Alexander Turnbull Library, S. C. Smith Collection

in New Zealand in 1901, began his career as a builder's apprentice in Dunedin,
studied architecture in the United States then returned to Dunedin in 1907
where he quickly established a flourishing practice. Following his work there
on the New Zealand and South Seas Exhibition of 1925 he shifted his practice
to Wellington in order to be ready to design the New Zealand Centennial
Exhibition of 1939–40. His Hawke's Bay Farmers' Building is a three-storyed
structure built on reinforced concrete foundations with a similar superstructure.

It housed a large department store on its ground floor and the town's first
lift transported patrons up to a magnificently appointed tearooms and further
above, to offices. Anscombe gave Hastings a building worthy of Auckland or
Wellington, its first and second floor façades having the recessed windows,
darkened spandrel panels and prominent pilasters of many office buildings
built during the 1920s in those cities. Pilasters extend to parapet level to form
rhythmical groups along the façade thus accentuating the building's height.
Sadly, the interior spaces have seen frequent alteration; ceilings have been
lowered and polished Tasmanian hardwood obscured, particularly on the
ground floor. The original lift remains.

Sensing that this prosperous town would be likely to require his professional
skills in the future, Anscombe established a branch of his Wellington practice
in the Hawke's Bay Farmers' Building. The reconstruction period immediately
following the earthquake was to give unexpected justification to his decision.

As Mary Boyd pointed out in her history of the town, "in rebuilding
Hastings no one wanted to have anything more to do with bricks or multi-
storyed buildings." Thus St Andrew's Church lost its spire and St Matthew's had
its tower considerably lowered. The Post Office, whose tower had completely
collapsed, depositing its bells into the street, was temporarily restored without
a tower. The Fletcher Construction Company quickly built temporary banking
premises in both Hastings and Napier. James Fletcher, director of the country's
largest construction firm, counselled against over hasty rebuilding and
offered his services to the Prime Minister, George Forbes, in order to assist
in the reconstruction. His firm, local builders H. W. Abbott and the Edwards
Construction Company built many of the town's new shops, often, as Fletcher
pointed out, making no profit whatever.

The bulk of the architectural work was done by an association of architects
formed, as at Napier, across normal professional boundaries, to see to the

efficient replacement of damaged premises. Among its Hastings members were the firms of Davies, Garnett and Phillips; Edmund Anscombe and Associates and other architects from Napier, Wellington and Auckland.

Initially the work involved the demolition of wrecked buildings and the carrying out of essential repairs to damaged ones. It was not until 1933–34 that substantial numbers of new buildings began to appear fully completed in the town's central business district. As at nearby Napier architects tended to design conventionally planned office and business premises whose distinguishing factor was the exterior use of Spanish Mission or Art Deco styling. It is this more than anything else which has made both towns internationally known among enthusiasts for 1930s architecture. Hastings has a pedigree of Spanish Mission buildings which pre-dates the 1931 earthquake.

It is significant that Hastings also has a number of fine Art Deco buildings equally as interesting as those in Napier and in some places forming a more cohesive, block-long sequence. It is interesting, too, that the decoration on Hastings' Art Deco façades tends to be more confidently appied than in Napier.

The most immediately arresting of the new Hastings commercial premises was the department store Anscombe designed for Westerman & Co in 1932. Like all other post-earthquake buildings it was built entirely of reinforced concrete with the exception of one cavity brick wall. The architect seized the opportunity of a highly visible site at the corner of Russell and Heretaunga Streets to add something of his own to the Spanish Mission character of Hastings. Westerman's, established in 1910, was one of the town's oldest firms.

The company's 1921 building on the same site had been completely destroyed in the earthquake but fortunately many of its interior fittings, including a magnificent wooden staircase purportedly designed by Albert Garnett, were able to be reused in the new building.

Anscombe divided the longer Russell Street elevation into three sections along which he used a number of highly characterful Spanish Mission features On the shorter Heretaunga Street elevation he flanked a group of three round-headed windows with a pair of square-headed ones capped with decorative mouldings. The splayed corner at the centre links the two elevations, drawing attention to its importance by means of a pair of French doors which give on to a balcony with a wrought iron balustrade. The doorway is framed with barley

The State Theatre (1933) was designed by Anscombe and Auckland architect Vernon Brown in association. Its layered ceiling with concealed neon tubing made it Hawke's Bay's most flamboyantly Art Deco cinema interior. The auditorium was divided into two when the theatre was converted into a multiplex in 1994.

At the opening in 1933 of Nathan & Co's building, tenants and construction workers assembled for a commemorative photograph. Why some of those pictured are wearing false noses remains a mystery.
Alexander Turnbull Library, Whitehead Collection

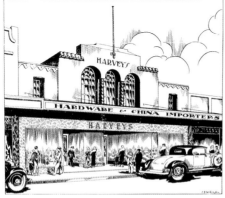

Colin Wilkinson's illustrations of the exterior and interior of Harvey's were reproduced in the commemorative brochure issued for the shop's re-opening in 1933.
Harvey Family

The Hastings Branch of the National Bank of New Zealand (1933) in Market Street. Designed by Atkins & Mitchell of Wellington, it was demolished c.1970.
The Hawke's Bay Branch of the Vintage Car Club of New Zealand

twist half columns and fluted Corinthian pilasters. The round-headed fanlight over the doors is framed by an elaborately moulded arch which is echoed in the frieze decoration above. A verandah with a highly embossed pressed metal ceiling is wrapped around both façades; the use of decorative lead lights in the glazing below is particularly impressive.

During the 1980s Westerman's was ill-used by various tenants who, failing to acknowledge the building's special character, covered its façades with unsympathetic signs. In 1991 an auction of the old shop's 1921 interior fittings passed them off to an unsuspecting public as Art Deco. Some of these have now found their way into a wine bar which, if not the ideal place to house elegant wooden fittings originally designed to display such things as women's frocks and furs, at least guarantees their survival in Hastings.

Anscombe's sympathetic restoration of the severely damaged buildings at Iona at Havelock North ensured that the Spanish Mission character which Rush gave them as far back as 1911 remained for the future. The buildings Anscombe designed in restrained Art Deco or stripped classical styles: Kershaw's and the State Theatre (in association with the Auckland architect Vernon Brown) in 1933, the Central Building in 1934 and the Dominion Restaurant in 1935 were obviously not commissioned by clients with large budgets. Such was not the case when in 1934 the architect was employed to build a large single-storyed homestead at Washpool, another large land holding on what was formerly part of the Maraekakaho Station.

Mrs Esmé Glazebrook had been a pupil at Iona; she was familiar with Tauroa, Arden and Te Mata, houses on which W. H. Gummer had allowed his familiarity with Californian Spanish influence to be displayed. The client decided to commission Edmund Anscombe, working in nearby Hastings, to design a house which, as Westerman had done, made use of the fully stylistic armoury of Spanish Mission. The house is a clever manipulation of an established architectural vocabulary, in a way none of Gummer's was intended to be.

It was built around a four-roomed cottage whose proportions were hugely extended. A long garden front elevation is dominated by a projecting bay with curved parapet and a group of three fan-lit round-headed windows separated by barley twist columns. To one side is an arcaded porch with three openings.

Angled cordova tiles and blind balustrading break the parapet line. Inside rooms are proportioned on a grand scale, many of them with elaborately moulded cornices and picture panels. Washpool is also justly celebrated for its magnificent gardens based on designs prepared in 1935 by the Christchurch firm of landscape gardeners, A. W. Buxton and Sons.

In central Hastings the enthusiasm for Spanish Mission building continued. Next door to Westerman & Co. on Russell Street, Harvey's, the firm of hardware and china importers, had impressive new Spanish-styled premises designed by Albert Garnett. An unusual feature of the interior of the shop is a central staircase ascending to a balconied first floor; this detail is said to have had its origin in Mr H. G. Harvey's enthusiasm for the department stores he visited in Paris during the First World War. When the shop was officially opened in time for Christmas 1933, customers were given copies of a commemorative brochure with an introduction in Maori and illustrated with drawings by Colin Wilkinson. Because of their shared architectural character Westerman's, Harvey's, Christie's and Swan and Lavalle's CML Building, which completes the group at the end of Russell Street, are the most important commercial buildings in Hastings' Spanish Mission cityscape.

Both Harold Davies and Eric Phillips contributed modestly to the Spanish character of Hastings architecture; their Hastings Methodist Church of 1931–32 situated opposite the Municipal Theatre adds considerably to the Spanish flavour of this particular area of the city. Iona Chapel of 1957 is a belated though undeniably accomplished addition to the tradition. Although Harold Davies designed a large house in Spanish Mission idiom in 1935 for the builder H. W. Abbott, it was never built.

In the 1930s Davies and Phillips were the chief exponents of Art Deco in Hastings. Heretaunga Buildings, a 1935 reconstruction of the 1922 classically detailed original building by Hyland and Phillips, is typical of their work. As *Home and Building* informed its national readership in November 1937, the two ground floor shopfronts, the House of Blackmore, a men's outfitters, and Alan Grant, Chemist, "offered considerable scope to the designer, and the materials involved – glass, chromium-plated metal, tiles or terrazzo – are capable of manipulation into a variety of interesting forms." Sidney Chaplin's 1938 premises for John Hill Ltd and the former Medical & Dental Chambers, now Las Palmas of 1935, designed by Davies and Phillips, also proved how enduring the smart Art Deco styling was. So too did their 1945 Crematorium.

The premises of Alan Grant, Chemist, and the House of Blackmore, tenants of Heretaunga Chambers, were dressed in the fashionable Art Deco manner by Davies & Phillips in 1935.
Home & Building, November 1937

Queen's Chambers (1932) by Davies & Phillips.
Alexander Turnbull Library, Whitehead Collection

The Commercial Bank of Australia building (1932), also by Davies & Phillips.
Alexander Turnbull Library, Whitehead Collection

Garnett, although no longer part of the partnership, designed the impressive Art Deco Carlsson Flats (now an office building retaining the name Carlsson) in 1933 and, in 1934 Holden's Building. Still active during the 1940s he was frequently called upon to design what can best be described as Spanish Deco houses which combined the pared back Moderne house with all the decorative details commonly found on Spanish Mission buildings.

In other buildings such as the 1932 Queen's Chambers and the Commercial Bank of Australia (now an office building), and the 1935 Karamu Chambers (now Esam Cushing & Co), Davies and Phillips designed modest two-storeyed buildings with a rounded corner, set-back windows and stripped classical rather than Art Deco detailing. The Government Architect J. T. Mair's 1932 Post Office, now the Hastings Health Centre, exhibited the same restraint which was obviously considered more respectable for banks, government and legal offices and doctors' premises. In 1925 a precedent for this had already been set by Wellington architect Stanley Fearn's former Public Trust building with its superbly detailed entry dominated by two double height Ionic columns.

S. G. Chaplin did not become a partner of Davies and Phillips until after World War II. In 1934 it was decided in Hastings to call for competitive designs for a town clock to be situated at the railway crossing in Heretaunga Street. The judges of the competition were to be Harold Davis and Eric Phillips. After a lengthy correspondence with W. H. Gummer, at that time President of the New Zealand Institute of Architects, on the dangers of demeaning competitions by offering inadequate prize money, S. G. Chaplin was awarded the first prize of 25 guineas. The clock tower was built in 1935 and it incorporated a new clock and the chimes from John Campbell's 1909 Post Office which the earthquake had fatally weakened.

Other architectural practices in Hastings preferred to decorate their otherwise modest buildings with Art Deco motifs. Davies and Phillips, the surviving members of a busy practice which had for many years numbered Albert Garnett among its partners, was Hastings' best known practice in the three decades following the earthquake. Its principal was Harold Davies (1886–1976) who as early as 1916 had designed an extraordinary Baptist Church for Hastings two years after having moved there from Wellington. The other partner was Hastings-born Eric Phillips (1897–1980), who had been employed by Hoggard, Prouse and Gummer in its Wellington office from 1914 and supervised the building of Tauroa for Gummer in 1915–16. Following service overseas during the First World War he completed the examinations for an associateship of the Royal Institute of British Architects in London and then returned to work in Gummer's Auckland office. In 1920 he joined Henry Hyland and Harold Davies in partnership and in 1924 won a national competition with his design for Napier's magnificent Public Trust Building. By 1936 the Hastings firm was known as Davies and Phillips, changing its name to include that of Sidney Chaplin after World War II when the young man who had served his articles there, returned. It was Harold Davies who had arranged that Chaplin spend the year 1925 as a junior draughtsman at Gummer and Ford's Auckland office.

In 1988 a Planning and Design Study by Beca, Carter, Hollings and Ferner correctly identified the architectural significance of the city's central business district. As a result, the then Hastings City (now District) Council decided to promote a Spanish Mission theme in order to encourage the redevelopment of older buildings in the centre of the city.

In an example of foresighted urban planning which could well be emulated in other towns and cities in New Zealand, the Council did extensive historical research and in 1990 published comprehensive architectural guidelines. Its intention and eventual effect was to encourage the owners of businesses to identify their buildings correctly, thereby ensuring that both painting and signage were carried out in sympathy with the individual building's architectural character within the context of the cityscape. The Council led the way with a public amenity building programme which showed how the choice of a Spanish Mission architectural design theme and use of appropriate materials could contribute significantly to rather than detract from the city's already distinctive architectural character. The town square area was subject to extensive improvements made according to this theme. The new amenity block opposite Poppelwell's featured a painted roughcast surface, sloping brick corner buttresses, tiled roof and tower with curved parapet, overhanging eaves lined with exposed rafters and a cleverly conceived system of brick-outlined blind arcading. Landscaping that included a central water feature and extensive paving was used to join the area between Karamu Road and Market Street bisected by a railway line.

This floral model of the Town Clock was made for the Hastings Blossom festival of 1956.
Alexander Turnbull Library

For their work in the central business district, the Hastings District Council and Beca Carter Hollings & Ferner received the New Zealand Planning Institute's 1991 Award of Merit. The award also recognised the physical changes which had been made in central Hastings; the pedestrianisation of a section of Heretaunga Street, traffic diversions and the encouragement of a Spanish Mission architectural theme.

The beginning of the new millennium again saw substantial revitalisation projects in the town centre. In 1998 Council adopted a new Landmarks philosophy placing high regard on protecting and preserving heritage buildings in order to retain and enhance the Hastings streetscapes that boast so many heritage buildings. The central water feature was modified, a performance area created and public art used to punctuate the area. The central art work, an aerial sculpture by Neil Dawson, now draws the eye skyward to the back drop of restored Spanish Mission and Art Deco buildings in the town centre. This revitalised streetscape that draws on landscape, history, art and architecture was nationally recognised in 2002 with a Creative Places Award from Creative New Zealand.

Hastings District Council's urban design focus promoting a philosophy that additions to buildings should be integrated with rather than separated from their architectural context will progressively result in the city's appearance acknowledging the existence of a tradition going back many decades.

New Zealand can ill afford to neglect its architectural past. In Hastings, a city where some of the country's finest architects worked, local body politicians have realised that this heritage must be nurtured and that awareness of history need not be an impediment to progress.

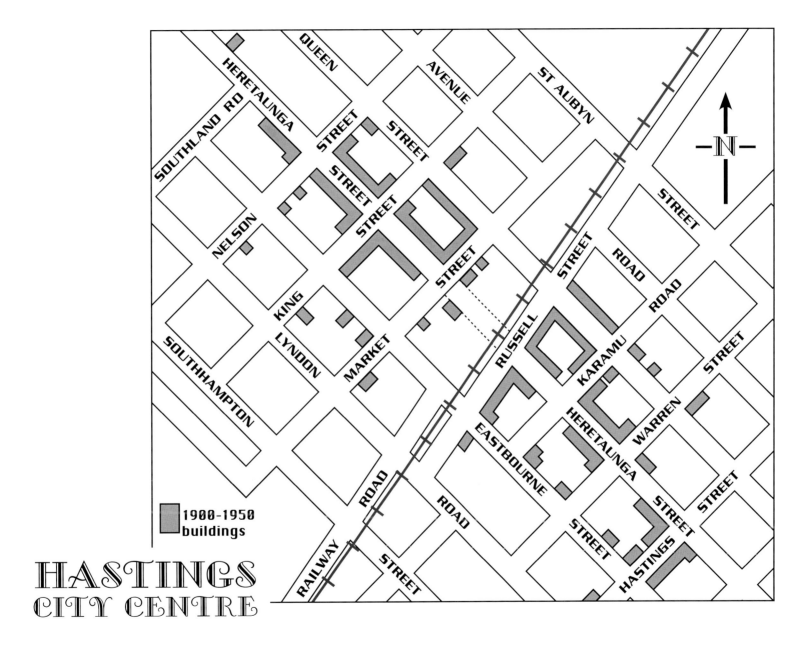

1900-1950 buildings

HASTINGS CITY CENTRE

33

Greenhill (1900) near Raukawa by George Sollitt. The house is
dominated by a three-storeyed central viewing tower to enable the
occupants to survey the Ngatarawa Plain below.

Glazed panel above an interior door.

Hand-painted stained glass door panels at Greenhill depict English pastoral scenes.

The guests' lounge is shaded by the surrounding verandah, its posts framing every view.

Part of the extensive panorama viewed from the tower.

The panelled hall and dining room are
connected by a folding wooden wall.

Above the stair landing is an example
of Art Nouveau glass fashionable in the
first decade of the century.

Called the Little Church of the
Flowers, the grotto-chapel at Matapiro
commemorates Walter Shrimpton for
whom the house was built.

Matapiro (1902–1910) by C. T. Natusch was built in
stages around a smaller original house. Its symmetrical
garden façade dominated by half-timbered gables hides
the complexity of the plan which is visible from the rear.

Tuna Nui (1912) at Sherenden by Natusch and Frankland. Exterior
walls of two-inch thick stucco and a tiled roof show that Natusch
was already moving away from his earlier practice of building large
wooden houses.

Kopanga (1912) at Havelock North by J. A. Louis Hay. Unlike other large brick or wooden houses by the architect, this huge concrete house survived the earthquake in 1931. The garden and drive were laid out by the Christchurch landscape gardening firm of A.W. Buxton and Sons who were frequently commissioned by wealthy landed Hawke's Bay families.

Whare Ra (1913) in Havelock North, by J. W. Chapman-Taylor, built as the home of Dr Robert Felkin, founder of the Order of the Golden Dawn in New Zealand.

The lower portion of the concrete rear elevation of Whare Ra houses the Temple of the Golden Dawn.

In this elaborately painted seven-sided vault members of the Order spent nights in meditation.

Glen Aros (1914) at Raukawa was designed by Albert Garnett who made early use of the Californian bungalow idiom. Substantial extensions at the rear by Judd Dougan Team Architects were added in 2001. Like many Hawke's Bay's homesteads, the house is now separated from the farm it once served.

Tauroa (1916) in Havelock North by W. H. Gummer.

A rear view of Tauroa clearly expresses the way in which the two wings radiate from the central circular stairwell.

Steps lead up to the roof from which panoramic views of the Heretaunga Plains are visible above each room.

The side elevation of Tauroa showing Georgian shuttered windows and Spanish Mission bell aperture set into the parapet.

An elaborate bronze light fitting decorated with a seated cherub is typical of the craftsmanship which is a hallmark of the house.

The inscription in beaten copper on the fire hood is similar to others in houses belonging to members of the Order of the Golden Dawn.

Tauroa's double curving stairwell is one of the country's finest.

Craggy Range, south-east of Havelock North, (1918-19) by W.H. Gummer. The architect provided at least two designs, one involving elaborate brickwork and the other in plastered brick. Elements of both seem to have survived when, for reasons of economy, the original owners significantly altered Gummer's designs. The house is currently known as Belmount.

The long pool is part of the garden laid out
by A. W. Buxton.

Arden (1926) in Havelock North, by Gummer and Ford, shows the architects' familiarity with the more modern Spanish influenced domestic architecture of California.

An external stair leads up to the roof on which it was originally intended to build a swimming pool.

Arden's Juliet balcony.

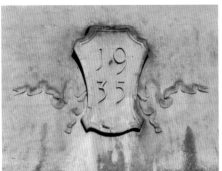

Te Mata (1935) near Havelock North by Gummer and Ford. The architects favoured a simpler Spanish-Georgian composition when they replaced the heavy Spanish-styled house which W. J. Rush had designed in 1920 and which collapsed in the 1931 earthquake.

The staircase at Te Mata, while less elaborate than the one at Tauroa, is beautifully lit.

Washpool (1934) at Maraekakaho by Edmund Anscombe. This is one of New Zealand's largest Spanish Mission houses. Inside the architecture reverted to an acceptable Georgian plan with classically-derived decorative treatment of cornices and supporting brackets.

50

The Anglican Church of St Matthew (1886) by C. J. Mountfort was extended in 1914 by the Wellington architect Frederick de Jersey Clere. Although it demonstrates the architect's advocacy of such modern materials as ferro-concrete and his adherence to Gothic principles, the result of the union with Mountfort's wooden church is unusual, despite attempts to unify the building's disparate sections with paint.

Inside, the concrete construction is clearly visible on the chancel's coffered, barrel-vaulted ceiling.

Among the chief glories of St Matthew's are the windows in the Lady Chapel, the work of the eminent English stained glass artist Karl Parsons. In 1914 he designed the five-light Adoration of the Blessed Virgin with Christ, Shepherds and the Magi.

Parsons added three smaller windows in 1926: The Virgin Annunciate, The Archangel Gabriel with the Annunciation and St Joseph, with The Flight into Egypt below. These are renowned for the intensity of their colour.

St Luke's Church, Havelock North (1912) by W.J. Rush, with its steeple added in 1998.

The chancel is all that survives of the work in 1881 of the eminent Christchurch architect B.W. Mountfort.

Iona (1913), Havelock North, by W.J. Rush was the earliest and largest Spanish Mission-influenced building in the district.

Iona Chapel (1957) by Davies and Phillips continued the Spanish theme.

Hereworth School in Havelock North, formerly called Heretaunga
School, was designed by W.J. Rush in 1913. The chapel in Hinerua
stone was completed in 1960 to designs by architect Ronald Muston.

Woodford House (1911) in Havelock North by W. J. Rush.

Opposite left: Davies and Phillips' Holland House (1934) at Woodford is somewhat unexpected given its architectural context however its subdued Art Deco appearance is in keeping with the times.

Opposite right: The Quadrangle, Woodford House.

Right: The Chapel of St Francis of Assisi, Woodford House, (1927) by Clere and Clere was sympathetically enlarged in 1968 by Wylde-Brown and Roberts.

Hastings Boys' High School's Frank Crist Building (1926) by George Penlington
continues the Spanish theme with its curved parapets and bracketed eaves
supporting a tiled roof.

Albert Garnett's classic Art Deco house in Pepper Street (1936), built for the jockey
Percy Atkins, was closely modelled on an almost identical house in Gisborne built
for Sir Robert Kerridge, Atkins' employer.

Rush Munro's Ice Cream Gardens. The
quirky cottage was built by Frederick
Charles Rush-Munro who started a
confectionary business in Hastings
in 1926 and moved it to the present
location after the earthquake which
destroyed his earlier shop. The
building is largely unchanged, and still
furnished with the quaint furniture
which he presumably made and
painted himself.

Part of a depression work scheme in
Hastings parks, this bridge was built in
Windsor Park in 1937.

The Hawke's Bay Opera House, Hastings (1914) by Henry Eli White
boasts the city's most impressive Spanish Mission frontage.

The boxes on either side of the stage were decorated with plastered and painted attenuated floral motifs similar to those used by designers of the Austrian Secession. These have formed the basis for the extensive interior decorative scheme added in 2005 by artists Roz Paterson and Tina Carter.

Henry Eli White despised "wretched pillars" that disturbed sight lines to the stage so he devised a steel framed cantilever system that resulted in only a single column being needed in the stalls to support the circle and balcony.

The plastered ceiling was decorated in 2005 with paintings by artists Roz Paterson and Tina Carter who made appropriate allusion to the building's Viennese influences.

The new decorative glasswork in the entrance doors is by John Owens.

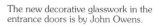

Harvey's Building (1933), originally a china shop and now the Hastings Community Arts Centre, by Albert Garnett. This owes its Spanish idiom to an agreement between the proprietors of Westerman's and Harvey's that their adjoining buildings should share an architectural character, hence the sloping cordova tiles, group of round-headed windows, barley twist columns and decorative railings.

The lofty interior suits its present role as an art gallery. The Art Deco glass laylight is almost identical to two laylights in Kershaw's Furniture Store in Heretaunga St.

Westerman & Co. (1932) by Edmund Anscombe and Associates.
In replacing the collapsed 1921 premises of the company Anscombe revived the town's Spanish Mission architectural
theme. Here the barley twist columns, round-headed windows and balconies are combined with classically derived details.
Westerman's verandah has a pressed metal ceiling and a variety of windows in stained and clear glass.

The building's interior wooden fittings survived from the original 1921 shop and were photographed before the department store closed.

Eastern & Central Community Trust occupies part of the upper floor of Westermans building. The fit out, by Pierre du Toit, utilizes and extends the original internal fittings.

The staircase is said to have been built to a design by Albert Garnett. Westerman's verandah is a pressed-metal ceiling and a variety of windows in stained and clear glass.

Hastings Methodist Church (1931–2) by Davies and Phillips picks
up the Spanish theme from its position opposite the Municipal Theatre.

Te Aute Hotel (1936), 32 km south of Hastings, was designed by Albert Groome. Unusually for the time, its late 1950s extension was carefully matched to the original building.

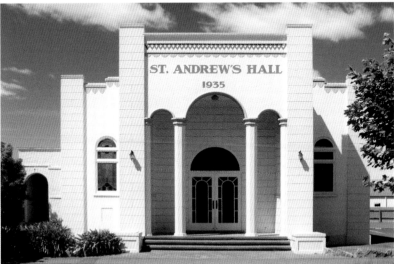

St Andrew's Hall (1935). Although its architect is not known, whoever was responsible was familiar with the Spanish Mission and Art Deco character of the newly restored town after 1931.

Poppelwell's (1924), originally premises of Fitzpatrick & Co, designed by Albert Garnett.
The eclectic mixture of Spanish and Stripped Classical idioms is clearly recognisable.

Villa d'Este (1929) shops and apartments by Albert Garnett.

Christie's Building (1934) by Albert Garnett.

The Russell Street Spanish precinct
concludes with Swan and Lavalle's
1929 Colonial Mutual Life Building.

The Municipal Building (1915) by Albert Garnett.

Hawke's Bay Farmers' Building (1928) by Edmund Anscombe and Associates (left). Built in reinforced concrete, it was a notable earthquake survivor.

This office building, formerly the Commercial Bank of Australia (1932) by Davies and Phillips.

The former Public Trust (1925) by the Wellington architect Stanley Fearn displays the classicism considered suitable for public institutions.

The Hastings Women's Rest (1920), reputedly the first amenity of this kind in New Zealand, was designed by S. B. Dodge, Hastings Borough Engineer.

Credit House (1914) is probably the work of Albert Garnett.

Little is known about the Dominion Buildings except that they were erected in 1908 for Lady Andrew Russell and were the first ferro-concrete building in Hastings.

The former Hastings Post Office (1932), now the Hastings Health Centre, was designed by the Government Architect, J. T. Mair. Like the Public Trust this large public building was designed in a more severe Stripped Classical style.

The former Bank of New South Wales by Crichton, McKay & Haughton, 1935. Its proportions, with pilasters whose capitals are decorated with ferns & flowers, were spoilt during the 1980s when a verandah was added.

Heretaunga Chambers (1935) was designed by Davies and Phillips, a reconstruction of Hyland and Phillips' 1922 Stripped Classical building. The new version replaced Classical detailing with Art Deco motifs.

Roach's Building (1934) by Harold Davies. Originally a department store, much smaller than the three storey one that collapsed in the earthquake, it was finished in natural grey cement, something rather unusual in a period when most buildings were coloured.

The Hawke's Bay Electric Power Board Building of 1912 (below) was probably designed by the Borough Engineer of the time. Its construction coincides with the Hastings Borough Council's first operating public power supply. The Power Board's 1938 building (right) was designed by Davies and Phillips. Its original terracotta tiled façade has been painted over.

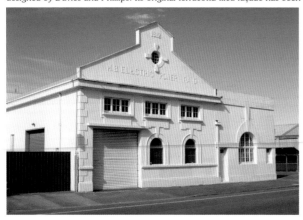

The former Ross Dysart & McLean's garage and showroom (1935) was designed by
Davies & Phillips. Like the Medical & Dental Chambers below, it utilised the architects'
favoured green coloured "block effect" with white faux pointing.

The Las Palmas building (1935), by Davies and Phillips, was built as the
Medical and Dental Chambers. Its streamlined rounded corners, metal windows,
projecting upper window and decorative outlining of edges can be seen on the
same practice's Crematorium (1945).

John Hill Electrical (1938) is the work of S.G. Chaplin. Corner-sited buildings made much of the rounded edges characteristic of Art Deco architecture. The building has been substantially altered since 1991 when this photograph was taken.

Above right: This small building in Nelson Street, also photographed in 1991, was Tong & Peryer's Funeral Centre, designed by Davies & Phillips in 1936. Its asymmetrical façade is quite unusual, a manifestation of the later Art Deco period.

Holden's Building (1934) by Albert Garnett is an Art Deco building whose appearance today is still compromised by a large sign structure above the façade.

Carlsson House, formerly Carlsson Flats (1933) by Albert Garnett, is one of the city's most accomplished Art Deco buildings.

Hastings Clock Tower (1934) by S.G. Chaplin. In this concrete structure hang the bells which were formerly housed in the Post Office tower which collapsed in 1931. Sculptor Neil Dawson's 'Suntrap' is suspended above the street.

The Dominion Restaurant (1935) was designed by Edmund Anscombe. The facetted glass probably replaces an original curved glass window, however after this went out of fashion it was impossible to obtain. The original signage remains above the shop-front.

The R&R Building by Harold Davies, of uncertain date in the 1930s, has an interestingly detailed curved corner elevation.

INDEX

Abbott H. W.   27 29
Alan Grant Pharmacy   29 **29**
Albert Hotel   6 **6**
Anscombe E.   13 25–28 50 64 71 77
ANZ Bank   9
Arden   19–20 28 **19–20 47**
Atkins & Mitchell   28
Atkins House   **59**
Atkins, Percy   21–22 59
Atkinson & Abbott   13
Auckland Grammar School   13

Bank of New South Wales (former)   **73**
Baptist Church   31
Beatson House   21 **21**
Beaux Arts   17
Beca Carter Hollings & Ferner   31
Belmount (see Craggy Range)
Birch, W.   5
Boyd M.   5 26
Brown V.   27–28
Burr & Mirfield   21
Burnham D.   16
Buxton A. W. & Sons   8 29 39 46

Campbell H. M.   7
Campbell J. (Govt. Architect)   9 30
Carlsson House / Flats   30 **76**
Carter, Tina   24 62
Cato House   21 **21**
Central Building   28
Chambers, Bernard   20
Chambers, Madge   16
Chambers, Mason   16–17
Chambers, Maurice   16 19
Chambers, Miriama   16 19
Chambers, Selwyn   10
Charlesworth J.   22
Chaplin S. G.   30–31 76–77
Chapman-Taylor J. W.   13–18 21 26 40
Christie's Building   29 **68**
Clere, F de J.   10 52
Clere & Clere   57
Clere & Williams   25
Cliff Press   10 **10**
Clock Tower   30 **32 77**
CML Building   29 **69**
Commercial Bank of Australia   30 **30** 71
Community of the Resurrection   14
Cornwall Park   59
Cosy Theatre, The   25
Cotterill & Humphries   10 **10**
Craggy Range   18–19 **19 45–46**
Creative New Zealand   32
Credit House   24 **72**
Crematorium   30 75
Crichton McKay & Haughton   73

D'Aronco, Raimond   23
Davies, Harold   22 27 29–31
Davies Garnett & Phillips   22 27
Davies & Phillips   29–31 57 66 71 73–77
Davies Phillips & Chaplin   31 55
Dawson, Neil   32 77

Dodge, S. B.   **72**
Dominion Buildings   72
Dominion Restaurant   28 **77**
Douglas, John   11
Dugleby W. A.   6–7
De Toit, Pierre   65

Earthquake (1931)   9 10 13 20 24–27 30–31
Eastern & Central Community Trust   65
Edwards Construction Co   27
English Free School   18
Esam Cushing & Co   30
Fearn, Stanley   30 71
Felkin, Dr R. W.   14–15 17 40
Fire Station   6
Fitzpatrick & Co   25 68
Fitzroy Street   21
Fletcher Construction Co   26
Fletcher, James   26–27
Forbes, George   27
Ford C. R.   19–20

Forerunner, The   11–12 14–15
Frankland F. H.   9 38

Gardiner, Reginald   13–15 17
Garnett, Albert
   21–22 25 27 29–30 41 63 65 68 70 72 76
Garnett, James   22
Glenalvon   **22**
Glen Aros   21 **41**
Glazebrook, Esmé   28
Grand Hotel   9 **9**
Greenhill   7–8 **34–35**
Gummer W. H.   16–21 26 28 30–31 42–46
Gummer & Ford   19–21 47–48

Hannah J.   24
Harvey H. G.   29
Harvey's Building   28 **29 63**
Hastings Blossom Festival   32
Hastings Borough Council   22
Hastings Boys' High School   25 **58**
Hastings Community Arts Centre   63
Hastings District Council   32
Hastings District School   5
Hastings Health Centre (see Post Office)
Hastings Hotel   6
Hastings Landmarks   32
Hastings, Warren   5
Hastings Women's Rest   **72**
HB Electric Power Board Buildings   **74**
HB Farmers' Building   **25** 26 **71**
Havelock North Town Board   13
Havelock North Village Hall   14 **14**
Havelock Work, The   13–14 16
Hay J. A. Louis   10–12 16–18 39
Heretaunga Buildings   29 **73**
Heretaunga School   13 56
Hereworth School   13 **56**
Hicks, Francis   5
Hill, John Ltd   30
Hoggard & Prouse   16
Hoggard Prouse & Gummer   19 30
Holden's Building   30 **76**
Holland House   57

Horonui   7 **7** 8
House of Blackmore   29 **29**
Hudson, Gladys   8 **8**
Hudson, Richard   8 **8**
Hyland, Henry   29 31
Hyland & Phillips   29 73

Iona College   13 **13** 28–29 **55**

James E. T.   11 13
Judd Dougan Team Architects   41

Karamu Chambers   30
Kerridge, Sir Robert   22 59
Kershaw's Building   28 63
Klimt, Gustav   24
Kilford & Ebbett   24
Knight Bros   6
Kopanga   10–11 16 **39**

Las Palmas (see Medical & Dental Chambers)
Lovell & Painter   4
Lutyens, Sir Edwin   16 18

Magdalinos, Paris   11
Mair J. T. (Govt. Architect)   30 73
Maraekakaho Station   7 21 28
Matapiro   8–9 **36–37**
McHardy House   12 **12**
McLean, Sir Donald   7
Medical & Dental Chambers   30 **75**
Methodist Church   22 **22** 29
Mountfort C. J.   9 52 54 **66**
Municipal Buildings   22 24 25 **70**
Municipal Theatre (see Opera House)
Muston, R   56

Nathan & Co   **27**
National Bank of NZ Ltd   **28**
Newbegin family   21
Ngawiwi   11
NZ & South Seas Exhibition   26
NZ Centennial Exhibition,   26
NZ Planning Institute   32

Oak Trees   15
Olbrich, Josef Maria   23–24
Opera House   22–25 **23–24** 29 66 **60–62**
Order of the Golden Dawn   14 17 40 44
Owens, John   62

Parsons, Karl   10 53
Paterson, Roz   24 62
Penlington, George   25 58
Penty & Lawrence   9
Pepper Estate   21
Pepper Street   21 59
Phillips, Eric   22 27 29–31
Poppelwell's Building   25 31 **68**
Post Office   6 9 **9** 22 26 **26** 30 **73** 77
Poukawa   11
Poukawa Station   7
Public Trust, Hastings   30 **71** 73
Public Trust, Napier   31

Queen Elizabeth, the Queen Mother   8 **8**
Queen's Chambers   30 **30**

Raukawa   7 21
Redwood, Archbishop   7
Rest House, Havelock North   13 **13**
Roach's Building   **74**
Ross Dysart & McLean   **75**
Rush Munro's Ice Cream Gardens   **59**
Rush W. J.   11–17 20–21 28 54 55–57
Russell, Andrew   8
Russell, Lady Andrew   72
Russell, Sir Andrew   8

Sacred Heart Church   7 **7**
Secession House, Vienna   23
Shrimpton, Walter   8 36
Sollitt, George   6–8 34
St Andrew's Church   **8** 26
St Andrew's Hall   **67**
St Brigid's   **21**
St James' Theatre   23
St Luke's Church   11 **54**
St Matthew's Church   **6 9** 9–10 26 **52–53**
State Theatre, Hastings   **27** 28
State Theatre, Sydney   23
Stoneycroft   **5**
Sunborne   15 **15**
Swan & Lavalle   29 69

Tanner, Thomas   5 6
Tauroa   14 **16–17** 16–19 28 31 **42–44**
Te Mahanga   11 **11**
Te Mata   19–21 **20–21** 28 **48–49**
Tong & Peryer's Funeral Centre   **76**
Torran   21
Tourist Motors & Farming Co Ltd   **22**
Tuna Nui   9 **38**
Turama   15
Tukituki Station   18

Union Bank of Australia   9
Upmeads (UK)   18

Van Asch, William   18
Vautier C. A.   9
Velati-Bellini, Guiseppe   23
Villa d'Este   25 **25 68**
Voysey C. F. A.   12

Waiterenui   7
Warren & Mahony   11
Warren R.   24
Washpool   28–29 **50–51**
Westerman & Co   13 **26** 27–29 63 **64–65**
Whare Ra   27–29 **40**
White, Henry Eli   22–24 60–61
Wilkinson, Colin   28–29
Wilson, Gordon   20
Windsor Park   59
Wood, Edgar   18
Woodford House   **12** 12–13 16 **56–57**
Wright, Frank Lloyd   10 18
Wylde-Brown & Roberts   57

BIBLIOGRAPHY

Boyd, M.B. *City of the Plains – A History of Hastings.*
Victoria University Press for Hastings City Council 1984

Grant, S.W. *Havelock North from Village to Borough 1860–1952.*
Hawke's Bay Newspapers Ltd 1978

Grant S.W. *In Other Days – A History of the Chambers Family of Te Mata.*
Central Hawke's Bay Printers and Publishers, Waipukurau 1980.

McGregor, Robert. *The Great Quake.*
Regional Publications Ltd, Napier 1989

Morrison, Robin. *Images of a House.*
Alister Taylor 1978

Shaw. Peter and Hallett, Peter. *Art Deco Napier – Styles of the Thirties.*
Reed Methuen 1987, Fifth Edition – Art Deco Trust 2002

Shaw, Peter. *A History of New Zealand Architecture.*
Hodder Moa Beckett 2003

Tipples, Rupert. *Colonial Landscape Gardener – Alfred Buxton of Christchurch.*
New Zealand 1872–1950.
Department of Horticulture and Landscape, Lincoln College, Canterbury 1989.

Waite, Paul. *In The Beaux-Arts Tradition, William Gummer Architect.*
Hawke's Bay Cultural Trust 2005

Weitze, Karen J. *California's Mission Revival.*
Hennessey and Ingalls, Inc., Los Angeles 1984

Hawke's Bay Before and After.
Daily Telegraph Co Ltd, Napier 1981 .

Publisher's Note: Six photographs in the book have been digitally manipulated to remove inappropriate signage or intrusions.